ORIGAMI DINOSAURS for BEGINNERS

JOHN MONTROLL

DOVER PUBLICATIONS, INC.
MINEOLA, NEW YORK

Copyright

Copyright © 2013 by John Montroll
All rights reserved.

Bibliographical Note

Origami Dinosaurs for Beginners is a new work, first published by
Dover Publications, Inc., in 2013.

Library of Congress Cataloging-in-Publication Data

Montroll , John.
    Origami dinosaurs for beginners / John Montroll.
        p. cm.
    Summary: "Paperfolders can get prehistoric with this new collection by an international
origami master. Ranging from the very easy to the low-intermediate level, 24 models include
a tyrannosaurus, apatosaurus, peterodactylus, dimetrodon, quetzalcoatlus, protoceratops, and
other famous and lesser-known dinosaurs—all based on Montroll's single-square, no-cuts, no-
glue approach"—Provided by publisher.
        ISBN-13: 978-0-486-49819-5 (pbk.)
        ISBN-10: 0-486-49819-0 (pbk.)
        1. Origami. 2. Dinosaurs in art. I. Title.

TT870.M559
736'.982—dc23
                                                                                                    2013
                                                                                              2012019868

Manufactured in the United States by LSC Communications
49819003   2017
www.doverpublications.com

Introduction

Dinosaurs have fascinated children and adults alike. Here is a collection of favorite dinosaurs which include the Apatosaurus, Tyrannosaurus, and Stegosaurus. You can make scenes and displays of these prehistoric animals. All the models are original designs and are from simple to low-intermediate in level.

In this colorful collection, a photo of each model is shown. The models are relatively easy to fold. Each can be folded in under twenty steps using a limited number of basic folds. For the new folder, it is recommended that you fold the samples in the Practice Folds section. As you progress through the book, you will find many recurring themes and related folds.

This work is the precursor to *Dinosaur Origami*. Once you have mastered these you will be ready to tackle the more advanced, varied, and detailed versions.

The illustrations conform to the internationally accepted Randlett-Yoshizawa conventions. Origami paper is colored on one side and white on the other. The colored side is represented by the shadings in the diagrams. Origami supplies can be found in arts and craft shops, or visit Dover Publications online at www.doverpublications.com, OrigamiUSA at www.origamiusa.org, or Amazon at www.amazon.com.

Martha Landy has provided a wonderful introduction along with information on the animals. I thank her for her contribution.

Happy folding,

John Montroll
http://www.johnmontroll.com

Contents

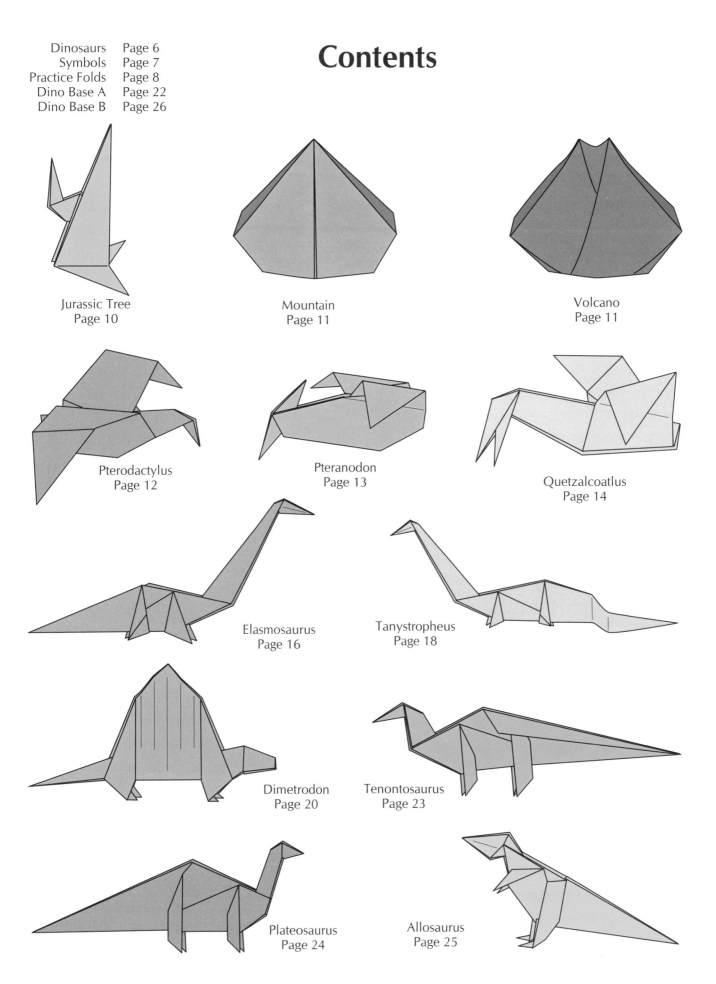

Jurassic Tree
Page 10

Mountain
Page 11

Volcano
Page 11

Pterodactylus
Page 12

Pteranodon
Page 13

Quetzalcoatlus
Page 14

Elasmosaurus
Page 16

Tanystropheus
Page 18

Dimetrodon
Page 20

Tenontosaurus
Page 23

Plateosaurus
Page 24

Allosaurus
Page 25

Contents 5

Dinosaurs

All dinosaurs lived in the Mesozoic Era. It began 225 million years ago and lasted for 155 million years. Each period of the Mesozoic Era, the Triassic, Jurassic and Cretaceous, presented different arrangements of the land masses and the seas. The differences in climate and vegetation allowed for different dinosaurs to flourish in each period.

Dinosaurs first appeared in the Triassic Period. It lasted for 45 million years. All the continents were connected into one giant land mass. There were only a few kinds of dinosaur and they were mostly small, quick carnivores.

The Jurassic Period began 180 million years ago. The continents began to move apart and shallow seas and swamps formed. The largest dinosaurs lived in this tropical climate.

It is the Cretaceous Period when we see the greatest variety of dinosaurs. It lasted for 65 million years. The continents were well separated although they were not where they are today. The earth began to experience seasons and flowers appeared on earth for the first time.

The continents have shifted since the Mesozoic Era. Paleontologists continue to hunt for fossil evidence of dinosaurs today. When a discovery is made the time period in which it lived as well as its location is important. This information can help scientists understand the habitat for a particular dinosaur and allow for theories about the dinosaur's behavior.

Martha Landy

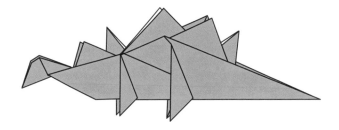

Symbols

Lines

— — — — — — — —   Valley fold, fold in front.

— · — · · — · — · · —   Mountain fold, fold behind.

————————————   Crease line.

························   X-ray or guide line.

Arrows

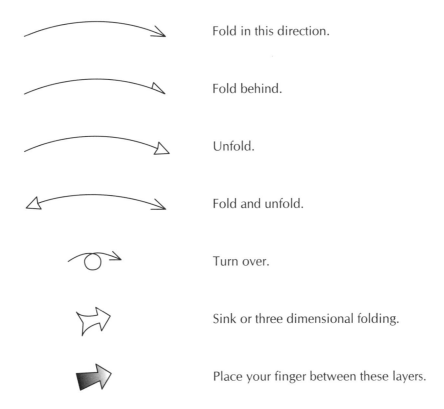

Fold in this direction.

Fold behind.

Unfold.

Fold and unfold.

Turn over.

Sink or three dimensional folding.

Place your finger between these layers.

Practice Folds

Easy Base

1

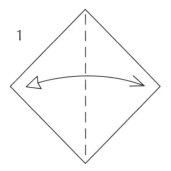

Fold and unfold.

Begin with the white side of the paper. Fold in half and unfold.

2

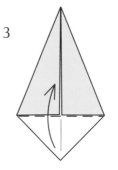

Kite-fold.

Fold two sides to the center to form a kite.

3

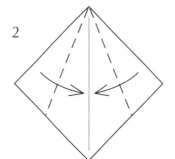

Fold up.

4

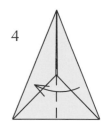

Fold in half and rotate.

5

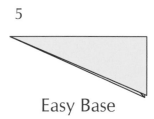

Easy Base

Reverse Fold

1

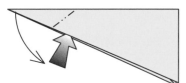

Begin with the Easy Base. Reverse-fold.

In a reverse fold, some paper is folded between layers. The shaded arrow shows where to place your finger.

2

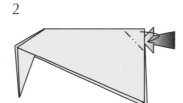

Reverse-fold.

3

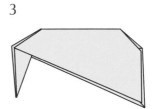

Practice Reverse Folds

Squash Fold

1

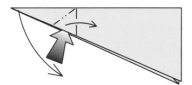

Begin with the Easy Base. Squash-fold.

In a squash fold, some paper is opened and then made flat.

2

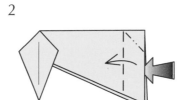

Squash-fold.

3

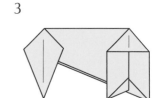

Practice Squash Folds

Crimp Fold

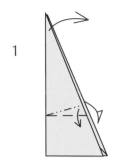

1

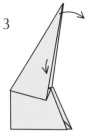

2

3

4

Begin with the Easy Base.
Crimp-fold.

A 3D intermediate step.

Crimp-fold.

Practice
Crimp Folds

A crimp fold is a combination
of two reverse folds. Open the
model slightly to form the
crimp evenly on each side.

Fish Base

The Fish Base is used for the Jurassic Tree. Also, many dinosaur
models use the kite-fold, squash-fold, and fold inside techniques
used here. Two methods are shown, which yield the same results.

Note that steps 2 and 3 in both methods lead to the same figure in
step 4. These methods are used throughout this work so it is important
to be familiar with them.

Method 1

1

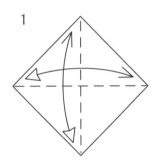

2

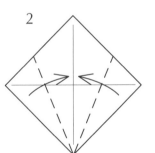

3

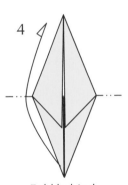

4

5

Fold and unfold.

Kite-fold.

Squash folds.

Fold behind.

Fish Base

Method 2

1

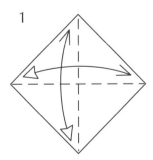

2

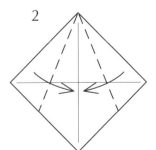

3

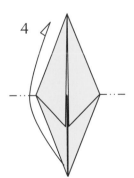

4

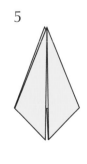

5

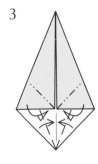

Fold and unfold.

Kite-fold.

Fold inside.

Fold behind.

Fish Base

Jurassic Tree

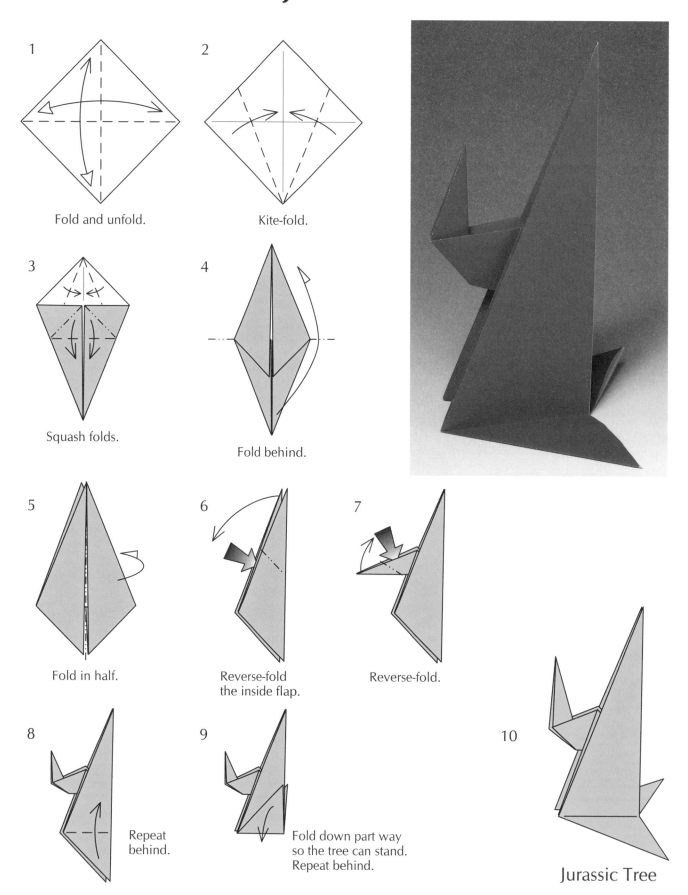

1

Fold and unfold.

2

Kite-fold.

3

Squash folds.

4

Fold behind.

5

Fold in half.

6

Reverse-fold
the inside flap.

7

Reverse-fold.

8

Repeat
behind.

9

Fold down part way
so the tree can stand.
Repeat behind.

10

Jurassic Tree

Mountain & Volcano

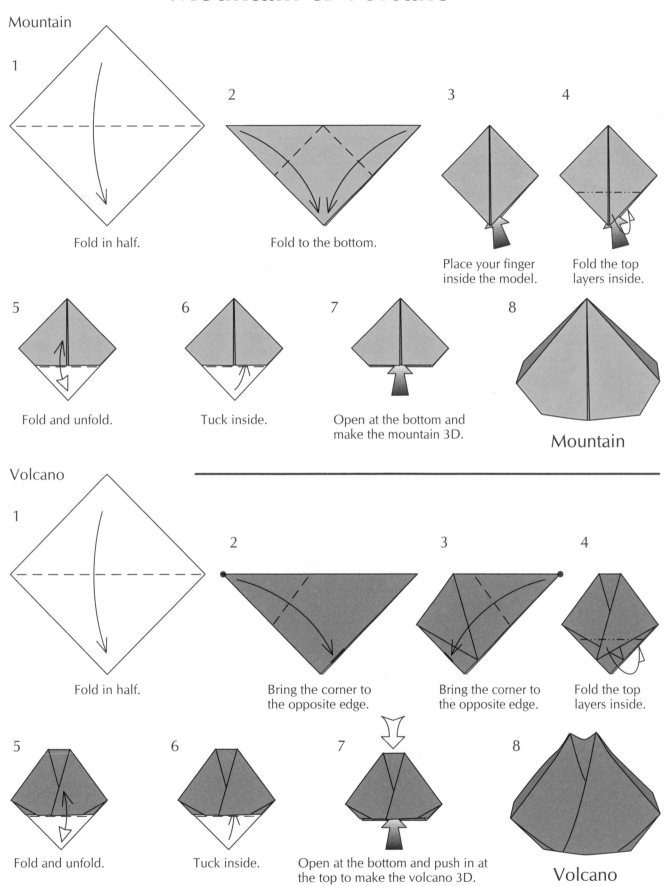

Mountain

1. Fold in half.
2. Fold to the bottom.
3. Place your finger inside the model.
4. Fold the top layers inside.
5. Fold and unfold.
6. Tuck inside.
7. Open at the bottom and make the mountain 3D.
8. Mountain

Volcano

1. Fold in half.
2. Bring the corner to the opposite edge.
3. Bring the corner to the opposite edge.
4. Fold the top layers inside.
5. Fold and unfold.
6. Tuck inside.
7. Open at the bottom and push in at the top to make the volcano 3D.
8. Volcano

Pterodactylus

ter-oh-DAC-til-us

Fossils of this Jurassic reptile
have been found in Europe.

1

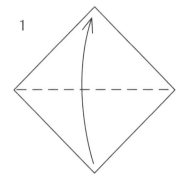

Fold in half.

2

Fold and unfold.

3

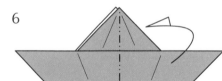

Fold to the center.

4

Unfold.

5

Bring the dots to the edges.

6

Fold behind and rotate.

7

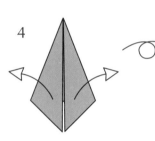

Fold through
the dot and
repeat behind.

8

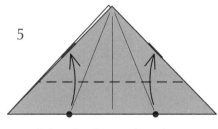

1. Fold the wings down.
2. Fold inside.
Repeat behind.

9

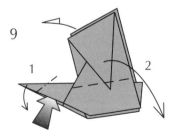

1. Reverse-fold.
2. Spread the wings.

10

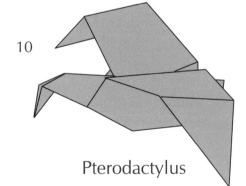

Pterodactylus

Pteranodon

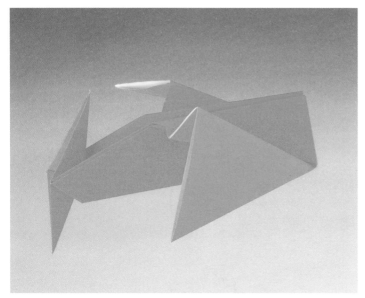

ter-RAN-oh-don

This reptile glided off Cretaceous cliffs in the Western U.S.

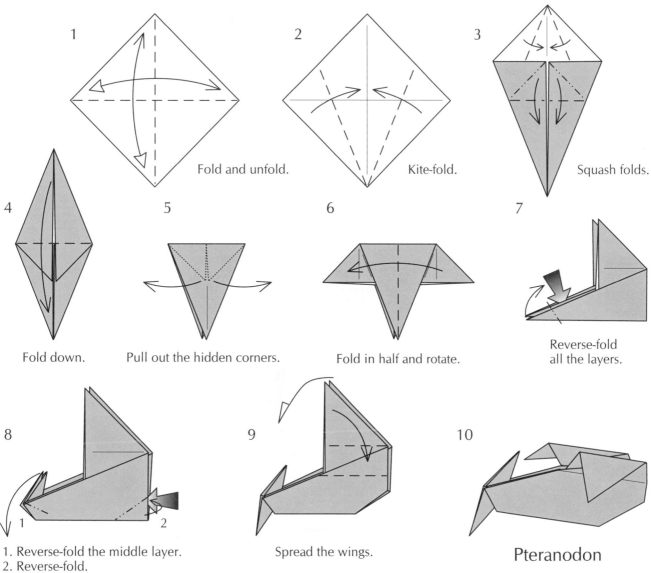

1

Fold and unfold.

2

Kite-fold.

3

Squash folds.

4

Fold down.

5

Pull out the hidden corners.

6

Fold in half and rotate.

7

Reverse-fold all the layers.

8

1
2

1. Reverse-fold the middle layer.
2. Reverse-fold.

9

Spread the wings.

10

Pteranodon

Quetzalcoatlus

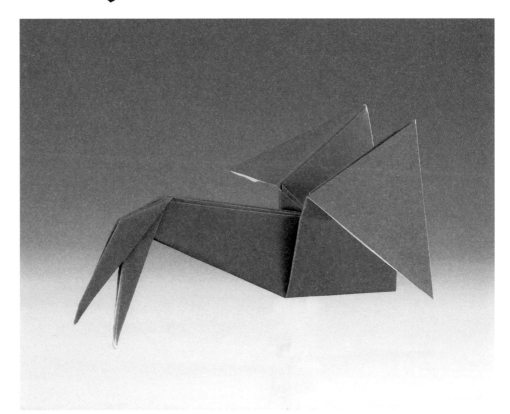

ket-SAT-co-at-til-us

This reptile soared over the Cretaceous sea of Texas.

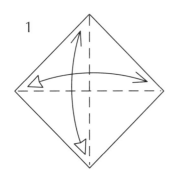

1

Fold and unfold.

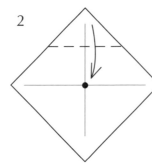

2

Fold to the center.

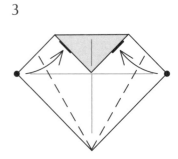

3

Bring the dots to the edges.

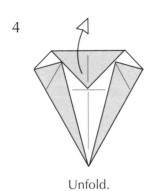

4

Unfold.

5

Squash folds.

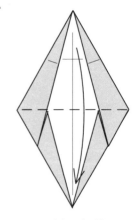

6

Fold in half.

7

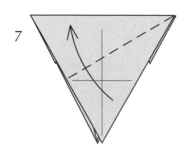

8

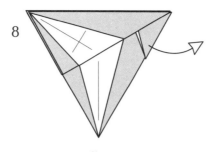

Pull out.

9

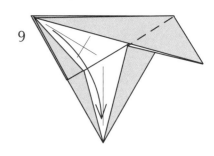

10

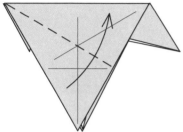

Repeat steps 7–9 in
the other direction.

11

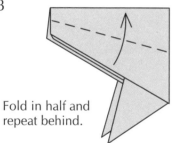

Fold all layers up a little
above the horizontal crease.

12

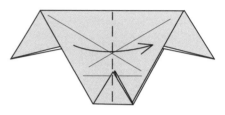

Fold in half and rotate.

13

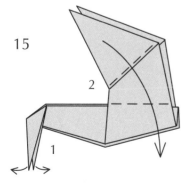

Fold in half and
repeat behind.

14

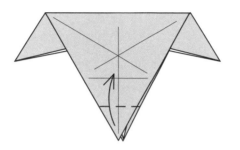

2

1

1. Pull the head down and
bring it to a point.
2. Fold the top layer back
and forth. Repeat behind.

15

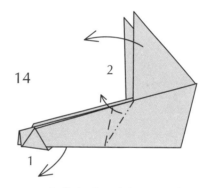

2

1

1. Spread the beak.
2. Spread the wings.

16

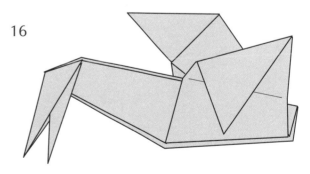

Quetzalcoatlus

Elasmosaurus

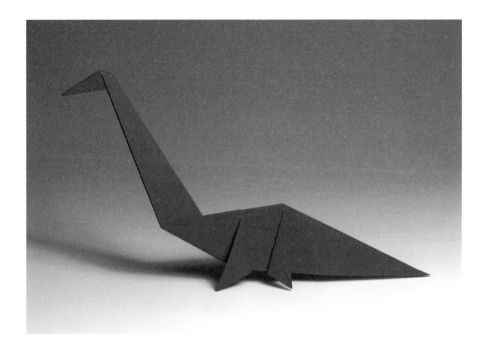

e-LAZ-mo-saw-rus

This marine reptile swam in the Cretaceous sea of Kansas.

1

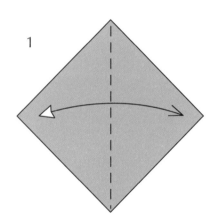

Fold and unfold.

2

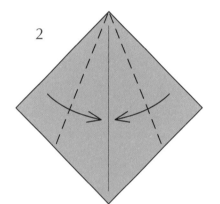

Kite-fold.

3

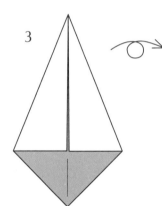

4

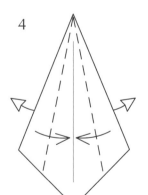

Fold to the center and swing out from behind.

5

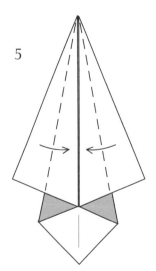

Fold to the center.

6

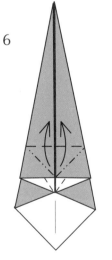

Squash-fold.

7

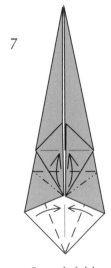

Squash-fold.

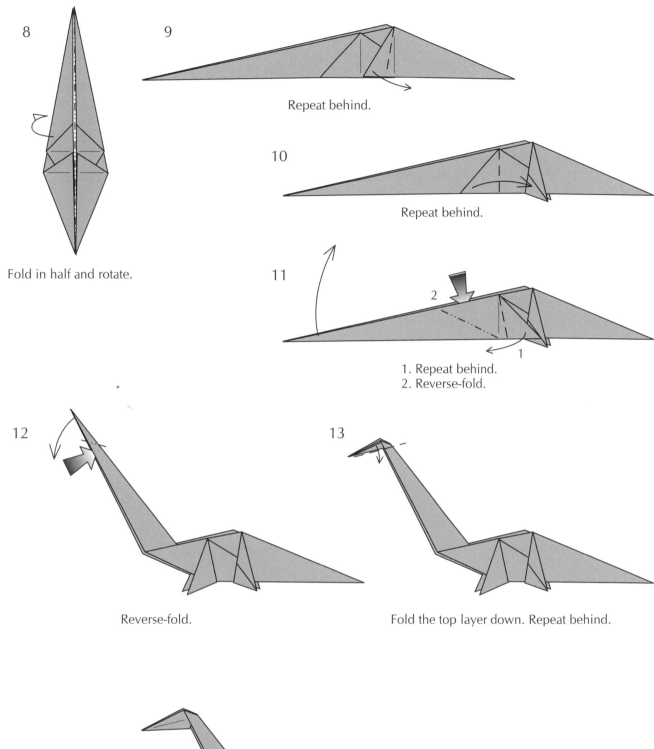

8

Fold in half and rotate.

9

Repeat behind.

10

Repeat behind.

11

1. Repeat behind.
2. Reverse-fold.

12

Reverse-fold.

13

Fold the top layer down. Repeat behind.

14

Elasmosaurus

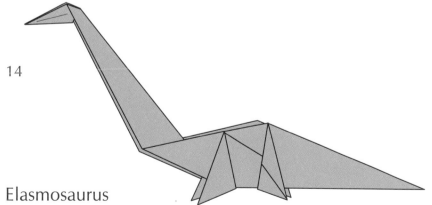

Tanystropheus

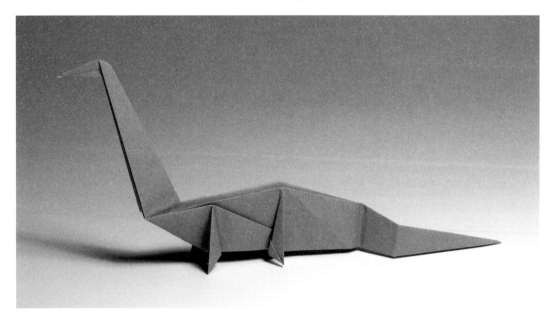

tan-e-STRO-fee-us

This lizard walked the Triassic seacoast in Germany.

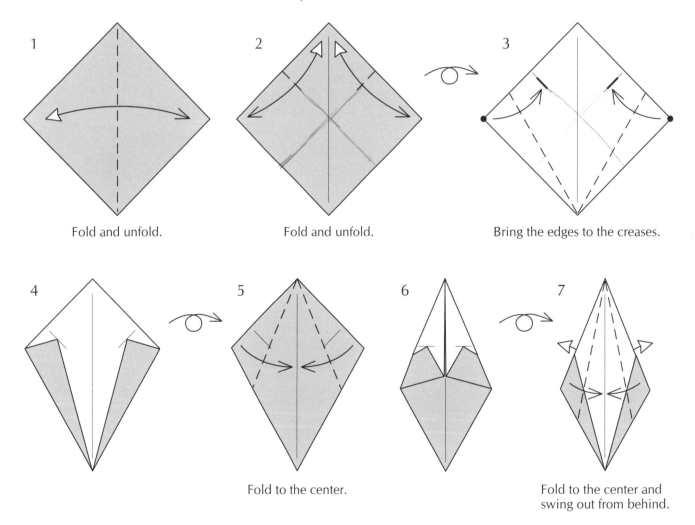

1

Fold and unfold.

2

Fold and unfold.

3

Bring the edges to the creases.

4

5

Fold to the center.

6

7

Fold to the center and swing out from behind.

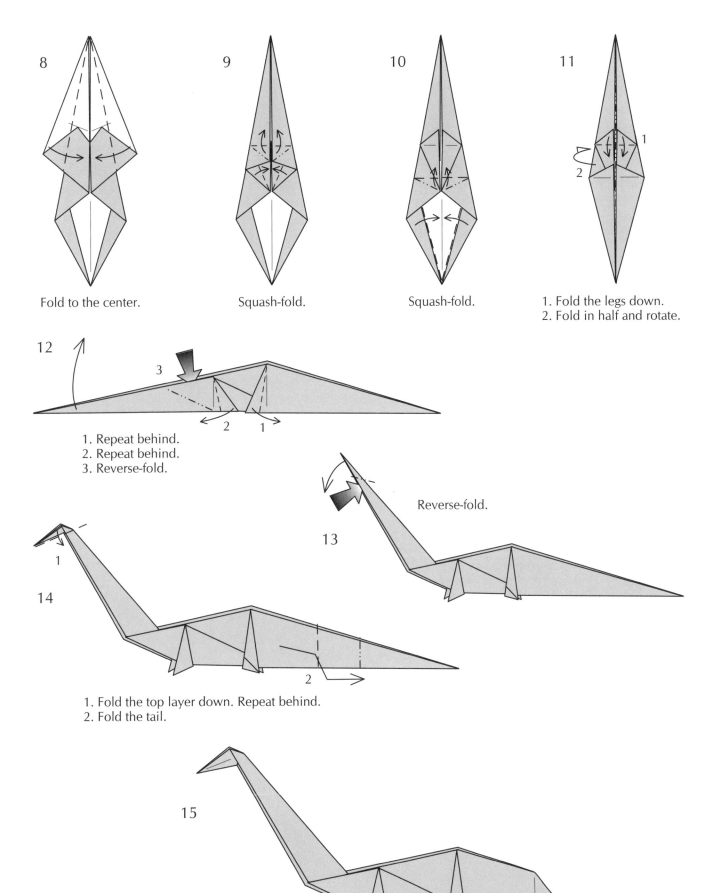

8

Fold to the center.

9

Squash-fold.

10

Squash-fold.

11

1. Fold the legs down.
2. Fold in half and rotate.

12

3

2 1

1. Repeat behind.
2. Repeat behind.
3. Reverse-fold.

13

Reverse-fold.

14

1

2

1. Fold the top layer down. Repeat behind.
2. Fold the tail.

15

Tanystropheus

Dimetrodon

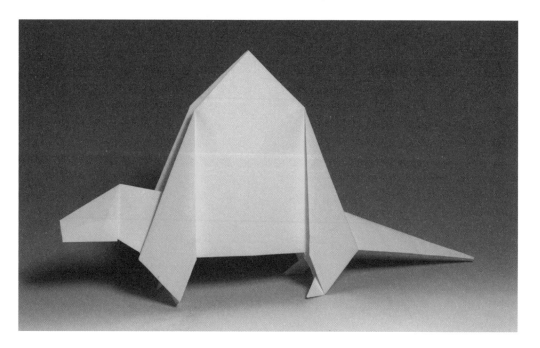

di-ME-tro-don

This reptile lived in Texas during the Permian Period.

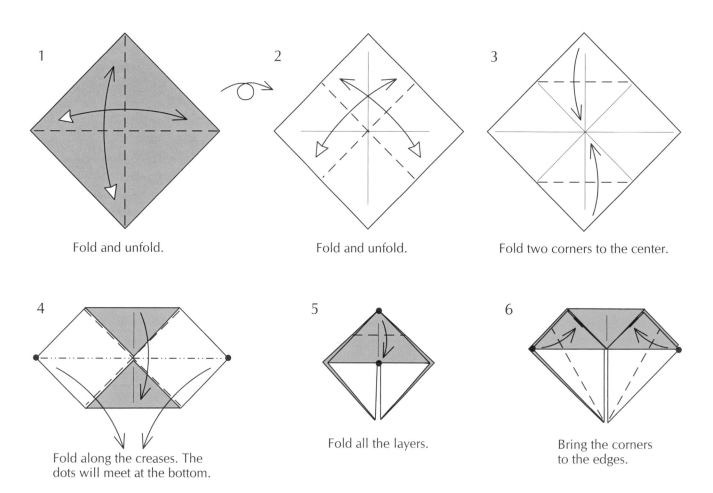

1

Fold and unfold.

2

Fold and unfold.

3

Fold two corners to the center.

4

Fold along the creases. The dots will meet at the bottom.

5

Fold all the layers.

6

Bring the corners to the edges.

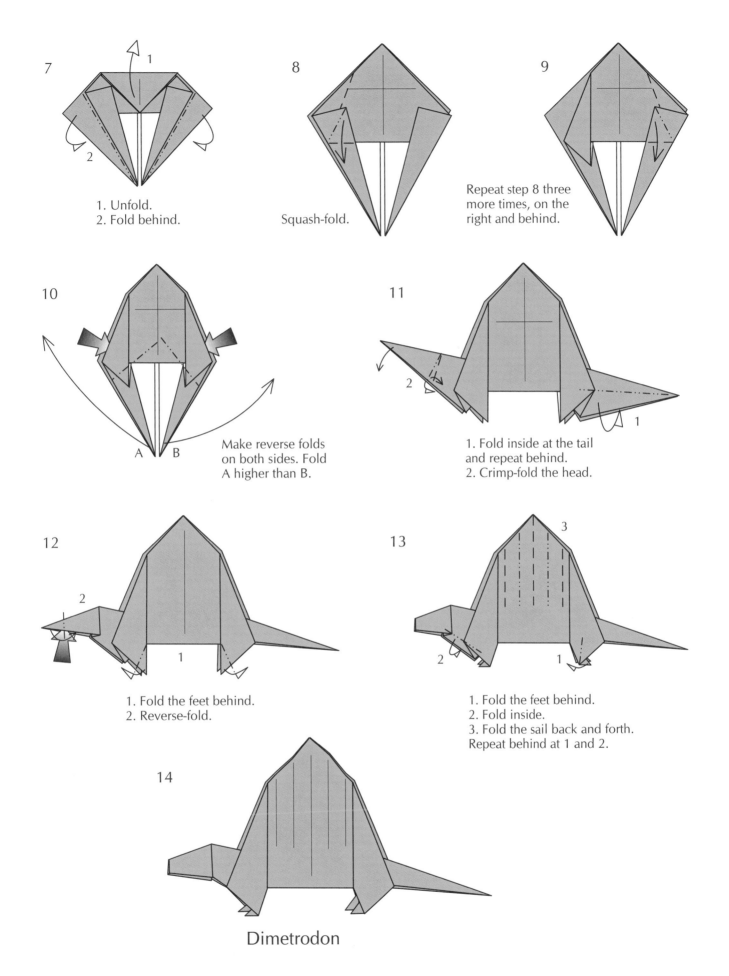

7

1. Unfold.
2. Fold behind.

8

Squash-fold.

9

Repeat step 8 three
more times, on the
right and behind.

10

Make reverse folds
on both sides. Fold
A higher than B.

A   B

11

1. Fold inside at the tail
and repeat behind.
2. Crimp-fold the head.

12

1. Fold the feet behind.
2. Reverse-fold.

13

1. Fold the feet behind.
2. Fold inside.
3. Fold the sail back and forth.
Repeat behind at 1 and 2.

14

Dimetrodon

Dino Base A

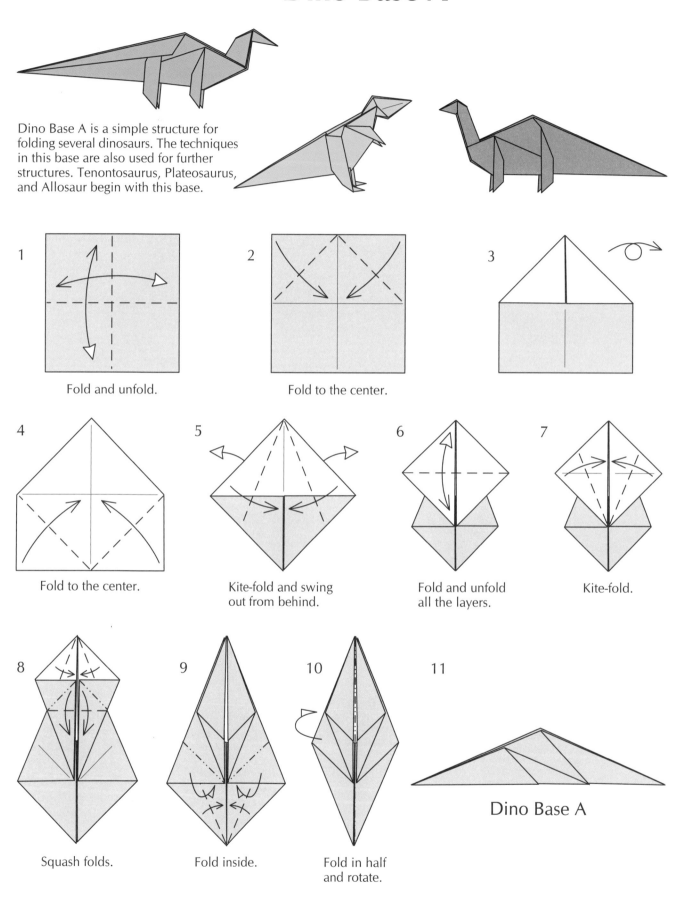

Dino Base A is a simple structure for folding several dinosaurs. The techniques in this base are also used for further structures. Tenontosaurus, Plateosaurus, and Allosaur begin with this base.

1

Fold and unfold.

2

Fold to the center.

3

4

Fold to the center.

5

Kite-fold and swing out from behind.

6

Fold and unfold all the layers.

7

Kite-fold.

8

Squash folds.

9

Fold inside.

10

Fold in half and rotate.

11

Dino Base A

Tenontosaurus

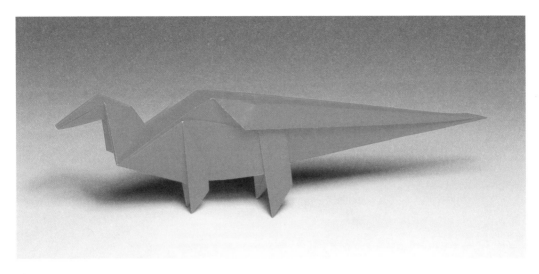

ten-ON-tuh-sawr-us

This Cretaceous dinosaur's fossils have been found in the Western U.S.

Begin with Dino Base A (on page 22).

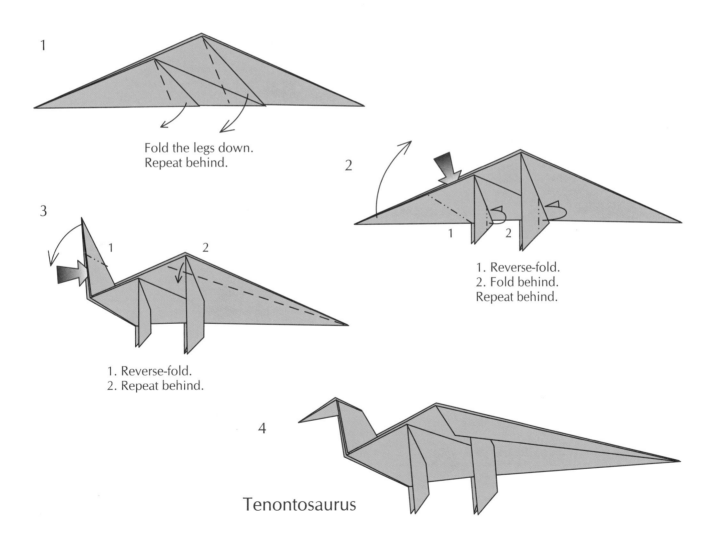

1

Fold the legs down.
Repeat behind.

2

1. Reverse-fold.
2. Fold behind.
Repeat behind.

3

1

2

1. Reverse-fold.
2. Repeat behind.

4

Tenontosaurus

Plateosaurus

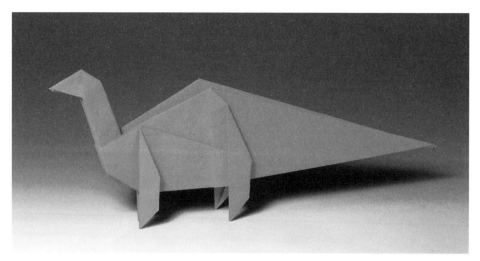

PLAY-tee-uh-sawr-us

Fossils of this Triassic dinosaur have been found in Europe.

Begin with Dino Base A (on page 22).

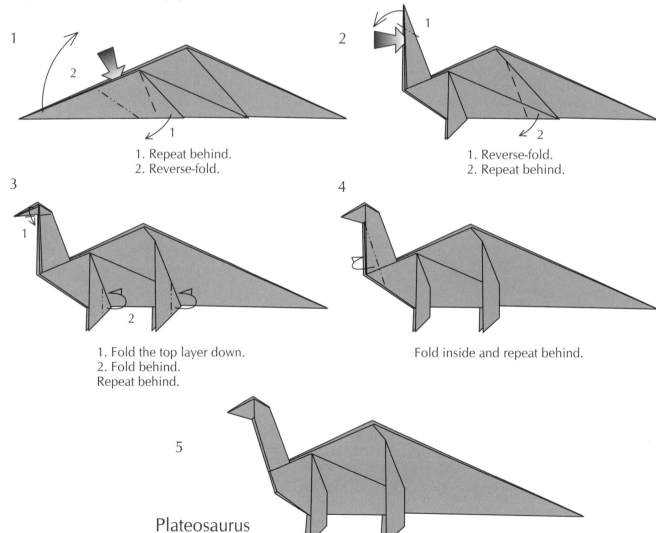

1

1. Repeat behind.
2. Reverse-fold.

2

1. Reverse-fold.
2. Repeat behind.

3

1. Fold the top layer down.
2. Fold behind.
Repeat behind.

4

Fold inside and repeat behind.

5

Plateosaurus

Allosaurus

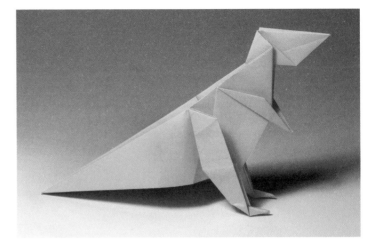

AL-us-saw-rus

During the Jurassic period, Allosaurus roamed Africa, Asia and North America.

Begin with step 10 of Dino Base A (on page 22).

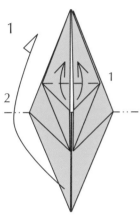

1

2

1. Fold in front.
2. Fold behind.

2

Fold in half.

3

Reverse-fold.

4

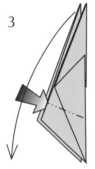

2

1

Note that the two dots are on the same line.
1. Repeat behind.
2. Reverse-fold.
Rotate.

5

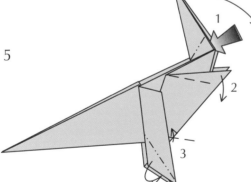

1

2

3

1. Reverse-fold the head.
2. Fold the arm.
3. Fold the legs in half.
Fold up at the arrow while
folding the leg in half.
Repeat behind.

7

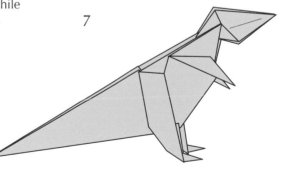

6

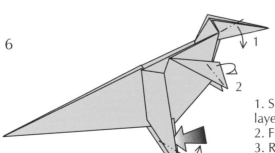

1

2

3

1. Spread the top
layer of the head.
2. Fold behind.
3. Reverse-fold.
Repeat behind.

Allosaurus

Dino Base B

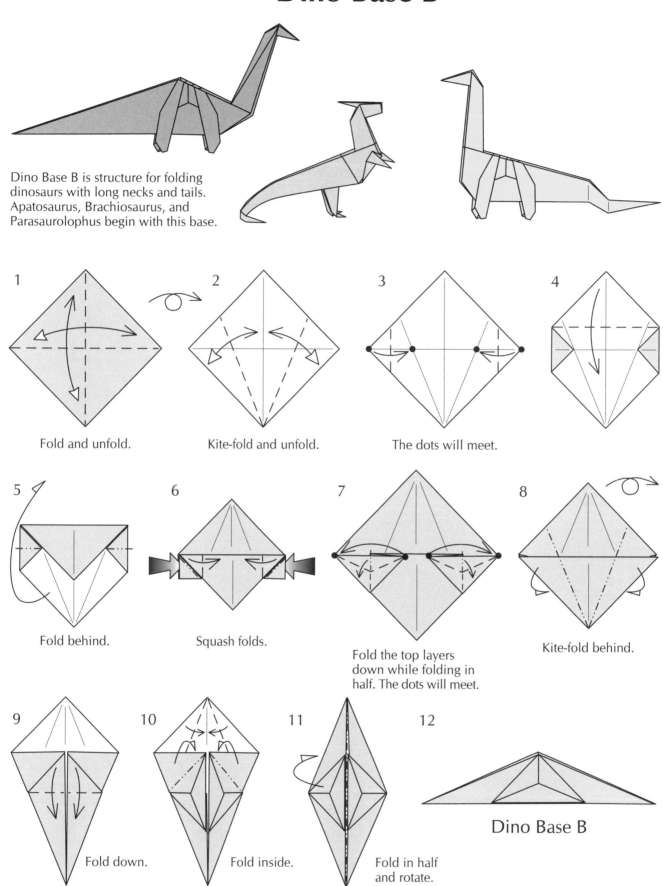

Dino Base B is structure for folding dinosaurs with long necks and tails. Apatosaurus, Brachiosaurus, and Parasaurolophus begin with this base.

1

Fold and unfold.

2

Kite-fold and unfold.

3

The dots will meet.

4

5

Fold behind.

6

Squash folds.

7

Fold the top layers down while folding in half. The dots will meet.

8

Kite-fold behind.

9

Fold down.

10

Fold inside.

11

Fold in half and rotate.

12

Dino Base B

Apatosaurus

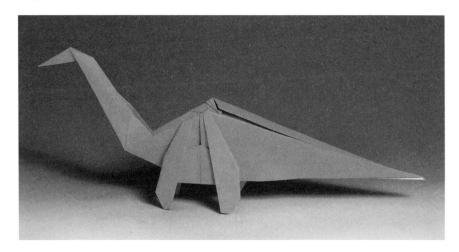

a-PAT-oh-saw-rus

Herds of Apatosaurus roamed the Western U.S. during the Jurassic.

Begin with Dino Base B (on page 26).

1

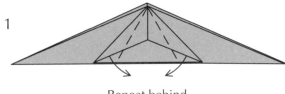

Repeat behind.

2

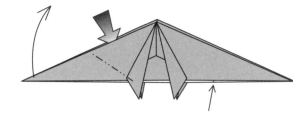

Note the layers at the bottom, right. Reverse-fold on the left.

3

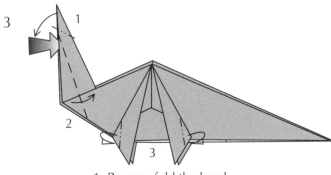

1. Reverse-fold the head.
2. Fold in front.
3. Fold behind on the legs.
Repeat behind (for 2 and 3).

4

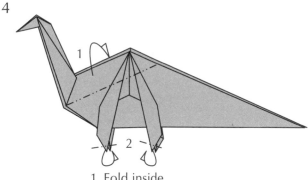

1. Fold inside.
2. Fold behind.
Repeat behind.

5

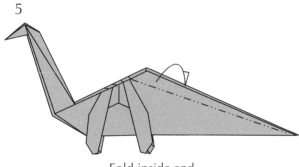

Fold inside and repeat behind.

6

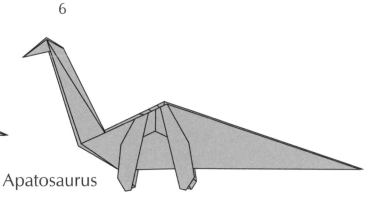

Apatosaurus

Brachiosaurus

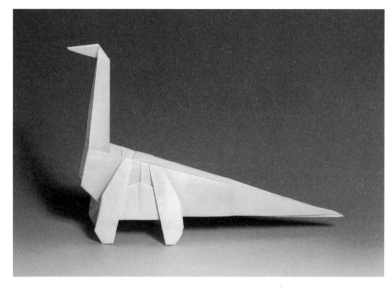

BRAKE-ee-oh-saw-rus

This dinosaur lived in the Jurassic period in what is now Colorado.

Begin with Dino Base B (on page 26).

1

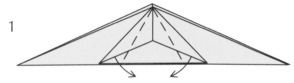

Repeat behind.

2

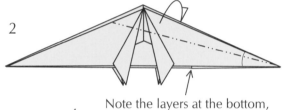

Note the layers at the bottom, right. Fold behind at an angle of about 1/3. Repeat behind.

3

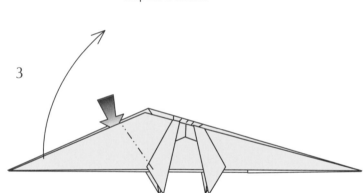

Reverse-fold.

4

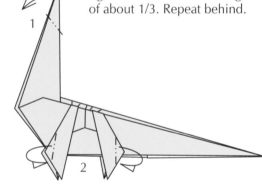

1. Reverse-fold.
2. Fold behind and repeat behind.

5

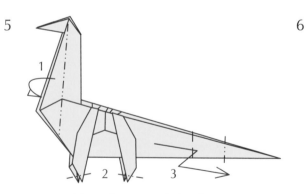

1. Fold inside, repeat behind.
2. Fold behind, repeat behind.
3. Bend the tail.

6

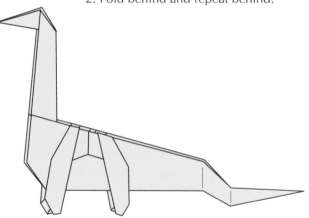

Brachiosaurus

Parasaurolophus

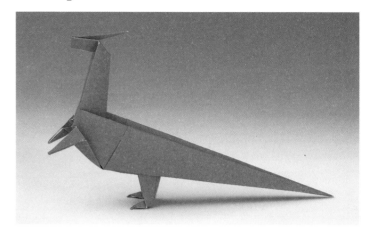

par-a-SAUR-oh-loaf-us

This Cretaceous dinosaur's fossils have been found in Western North America.

Begin with Dino Base B (on page 26).

1

Note the layers at the bottom, right. Repeat behind.

2

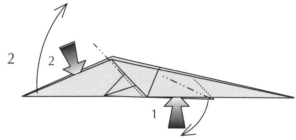

1. Reverse-fold the hidden leg to a point and repeat behind.
2. Reverse-fold the neck.

3

1. Fold the neck in half.
2. Fold the arm up.
Repeat behind.

4

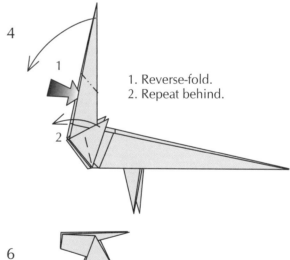

1. Reverse-fold.
2. Repeat behind.

5

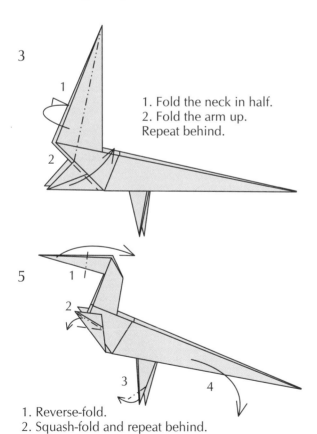

1. Reverse-fold.
2. Squash-fold and repeat behind.
3. Reverse-fold and repeat behind.
4. Curl the tail.

6

Parasaurolophus

Spinosaurus

SPINE-oh-saw-rus

This is a Cretaceous dinosaur and its fossils have been found in Egypt.

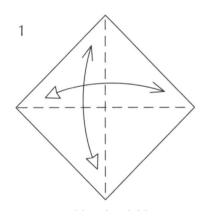

1

Fold and unfold.

2

Fold and unfold.

3

The dots will meet. Note the lower dot is slighty above the intersection.

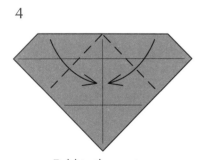

4

Fold to the center.

5

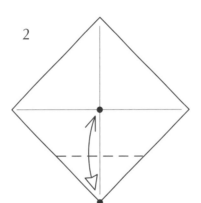

6

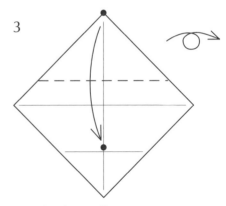

Squash folds.

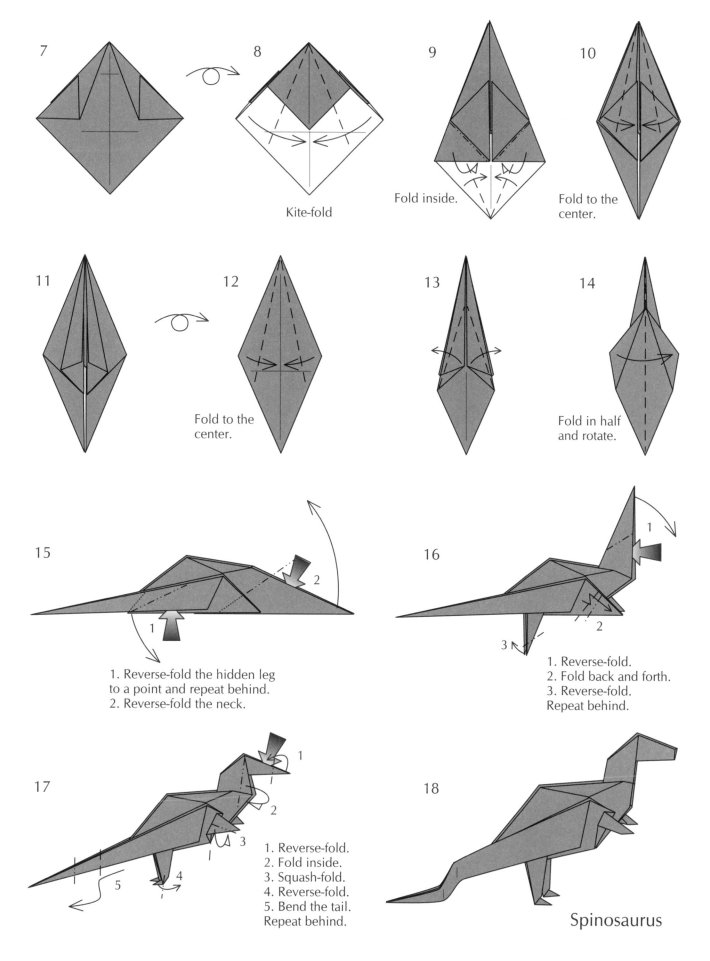

7

8

Kite-fold

9

Fold inside.

10

Fold to the center.

11

12

Fold to the center.

13

14

Fold in half and rotate.

15

1. Reverse-fold the hidden leg to a point and repeat behind.
2. Reverse-fold the neck.

16

1. Reverse-fold.
2. Fold back and forth.
3. Reverse-fold.
Repeat behind.

17

1. Reverse-fold.
2. Fold inside.
3. Squash-fold.
4. Reverse-fold.
5. Bend the tail.
Repeat behind.

18

Spinosaurus

Hypsilophodon

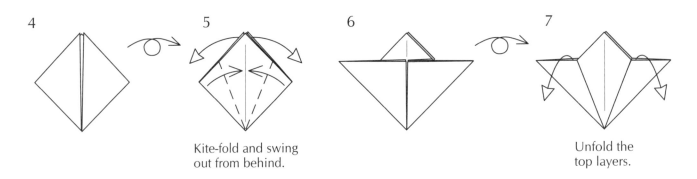

hip-sih-LO-fuh-don

Fossils of this dinosaur were found in South Dakota and the Isle of Wight.

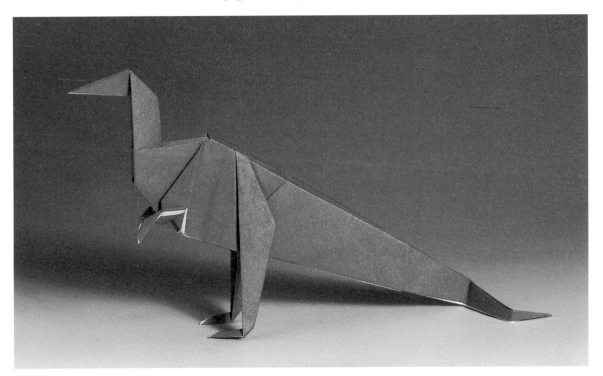

1

Fold and unfold.

2

3

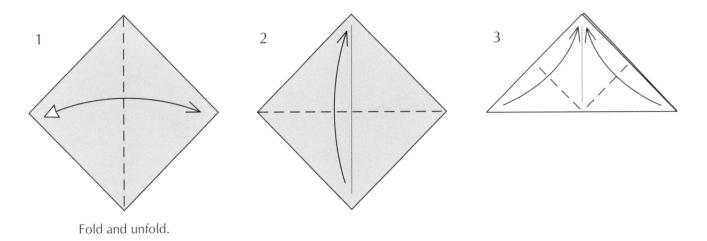

4

5

Kite-fold and swing
out from behind.

6

7

Unfold the
top layers.

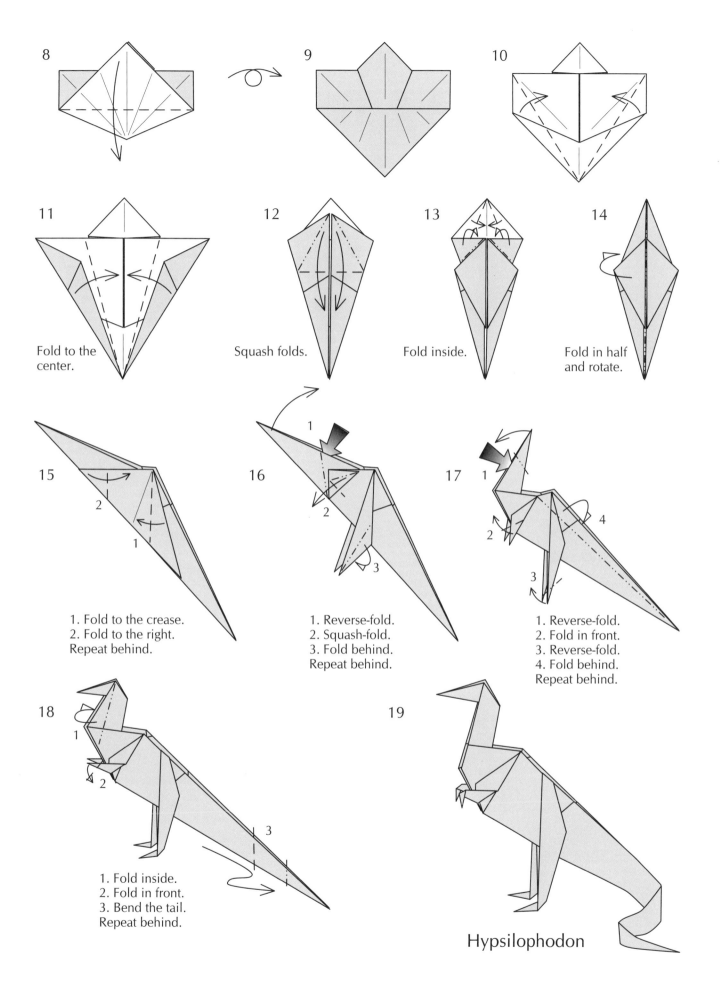

8

9

10

11

Fold to the
center.

12

Squash folds.

13

Fold inside.

14

Fold in half
and rotate.

15

1. Fold to the crease.
2. Fold to the right.
Repeat behind.

16

1. Reverse-fold.
2. Squash-fold.
3. Fold behind.
Repeat behind.

17

1. Reverse-fold.
2. Fold in front.
3. Reverse-fold.
4. Fold behind.
Repeat behind.

18

1. Fold inside.
2. Fold in front.
3. Bend the tail.
Repeat behind.

19

Hypsilophodon

Iguanodon

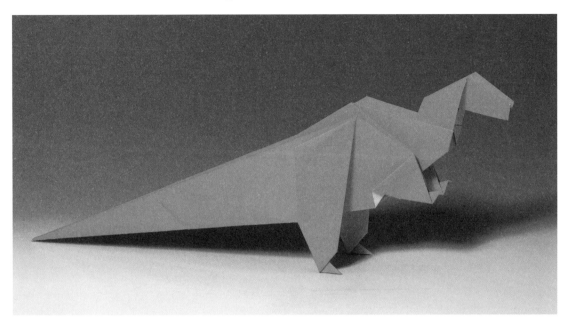

i-GWA-no-don

Fossils of this Cretaceous dinosaur have been found in Belgium and North Africa.

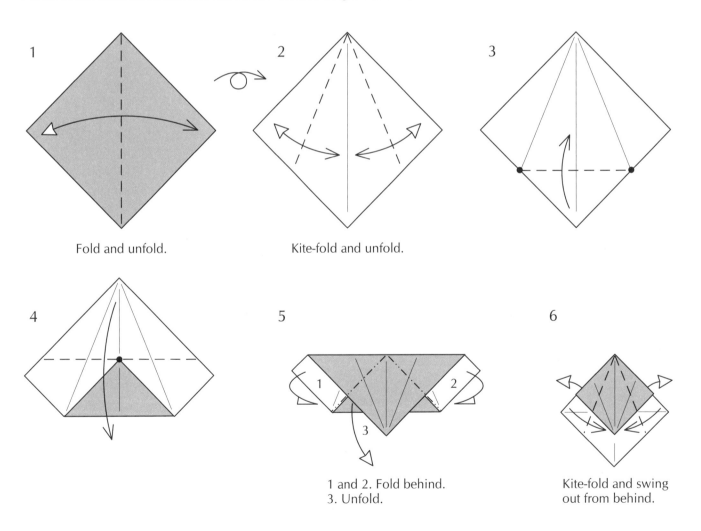

1 Fold and unfold.

2 Kite-fold and unfold.

3

4

5 1 and 2. Fold behind.
   3. Unfold.

6 Kite-fold and swing
   out from behind.

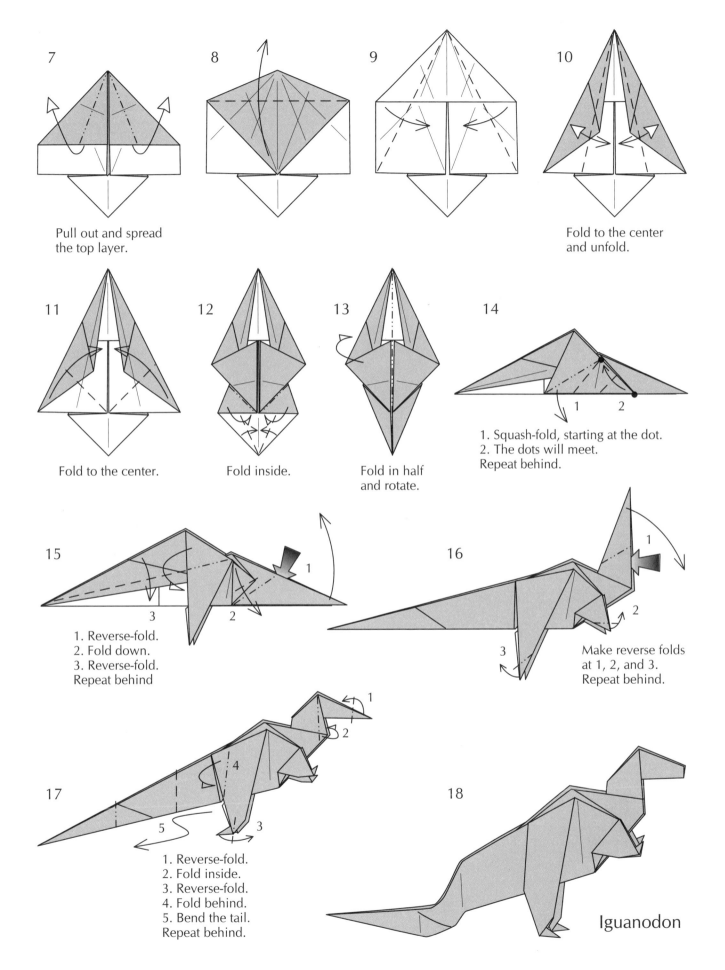

7

Pull out and spread
the top layer.

8

9

10

Fold to the center
and unfold.

11

Fold to the center.

12

Fold inside.

13

Fold in half
and rotate.

14

1. Squash-fold, starting at the dot.
2. The dots will meet.
Repeat behind.

15

1. Reverse-fold.
2. Fold down.
3. Reverse-fold.
Repeat behind

16

Make reverse folds
at 1, 2, and 3.
Repeat behind.

17

1. Reverse-fold.
2. Fold inside.
3. Reverse-fold.
4. Fold behind.
5. Bend the tail.
Repeat behind.

18

Iguanodon

Supersaurus

SOO-per-sawr-us

Fossils of this Jurassic giant have been found in Colorado.

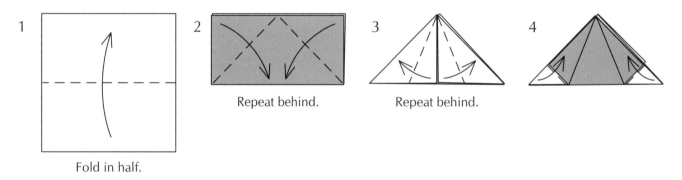

1 Fold in half.

2 Repeat behind.

3 Repeat behind.

4

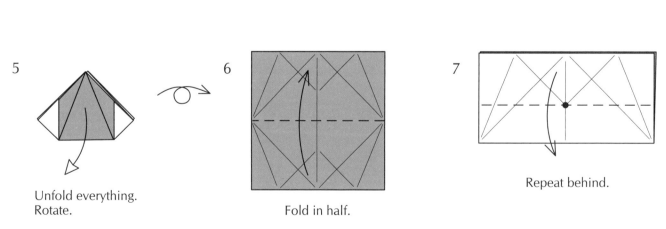

5 Unfold everything. Rotate.

6 Fold in half.

7 Repeat behind.

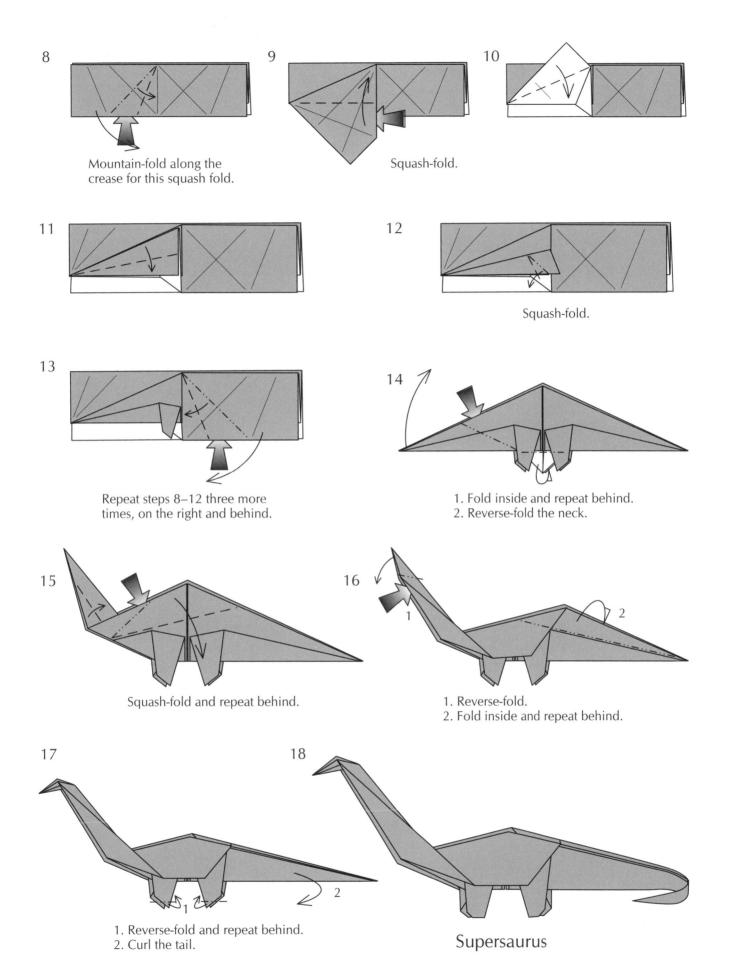

8 Mountain-fold along the crease for this squash fold.

9 Squash-fold.

10

11

12 Squash-fold.

13 Repeat steps 8–12 three more times, on the right and behind.

14
1. Fold inside and repeat behind.
2. Reverse-fold the neck.

15 Squash-fold and repeat behind.

16
1. Reverse-fold.
2. Fold inside and repeat behind.

17
1. Reverse-fold and repeat behind.
2. Curl the tail.

18 Supersaurus

Tyrannosaurus

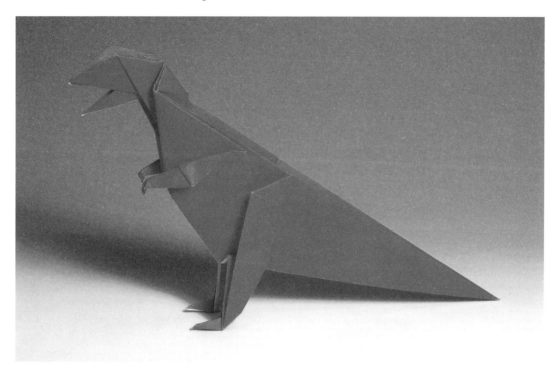

ti-RAN-oh-sawr-us

This Cretaceous dinosaur walked the North American continent.

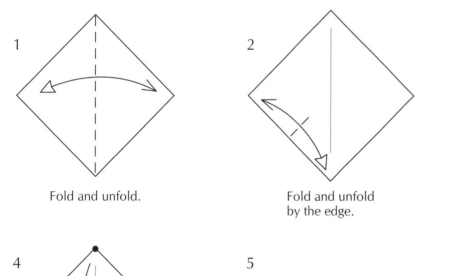

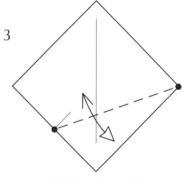

1

Fold and unfold.

2

Fold and unfold
by the edge.

3

Fold and unfold
by the diagonal.

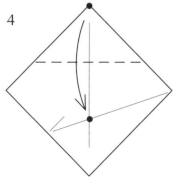

4

The dots will meet.

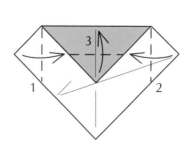

5

Fold in order.

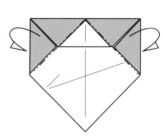

6

Fold behind.

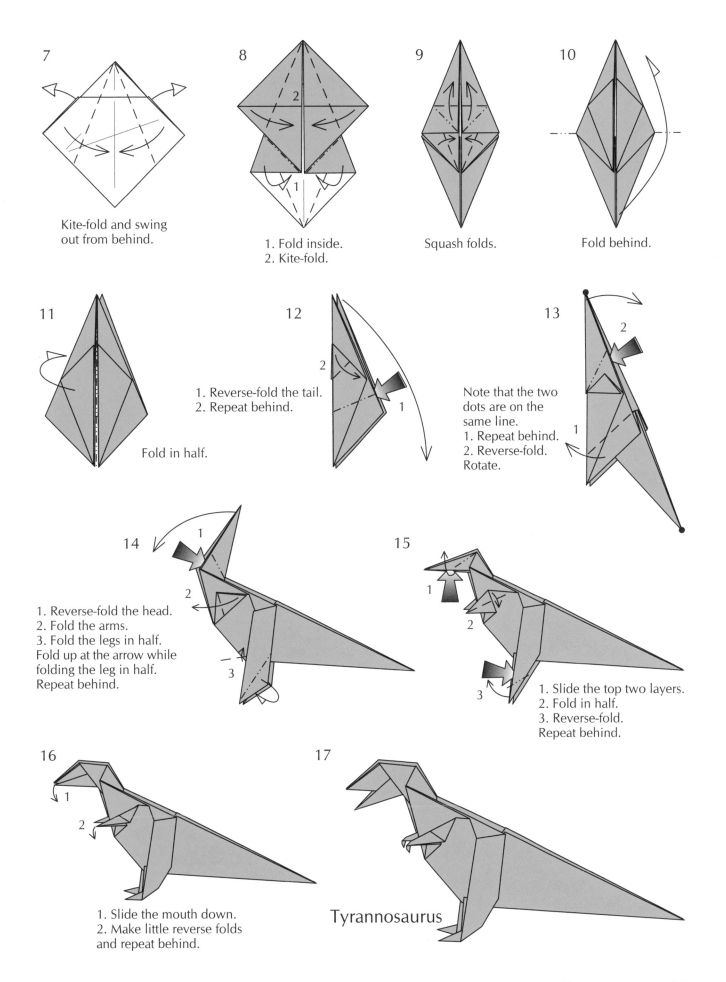

7

Kite-fold and swing
out from behind.

8

1. Fold inside.
2. Kite-fold.

9

Squash folds.

10

Fold behind.

11

Fold in half.

12

1. Reverse-fold the tail.
2. Repeat behind.

13

Note that the two
dots are on the
same line.
1. Repeat behind.
2. Reverse-fold.
Rotate.

14

1. Reverse-fold the head.
2. Fold the arms.
3. Fold the legs in half.
Fold up at the arrow while
folding the leg in half.
Repeat behind.

15

1. Slide the top two layers.
2. Fold in half.
3. Reverse-fold.
Repeat behind.

16

1. Slide the mouth down.
2. Make little reverse folds
and repeat behind.

17

Tyrannosaurus

Gorgosaurus

GOR-guh-sawr-us

This Cretaceous dinosaur roamed the Western part of North America.

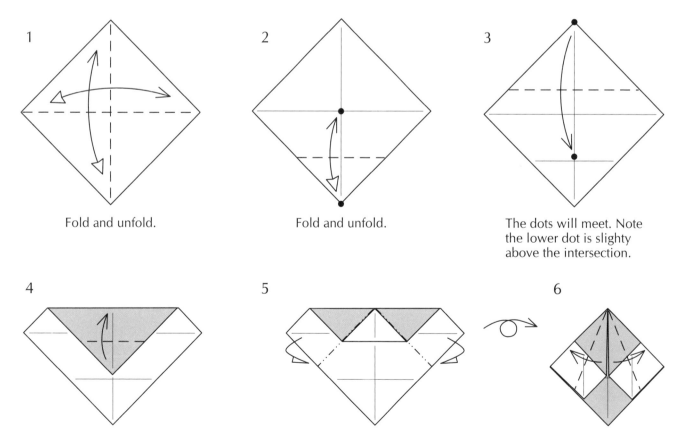

1   Fold and unfold.

2   Fold and unfold.

3   The dots will meet. Note the lower dot is slighty above the intersection.

4

5   Fold to the center.

6

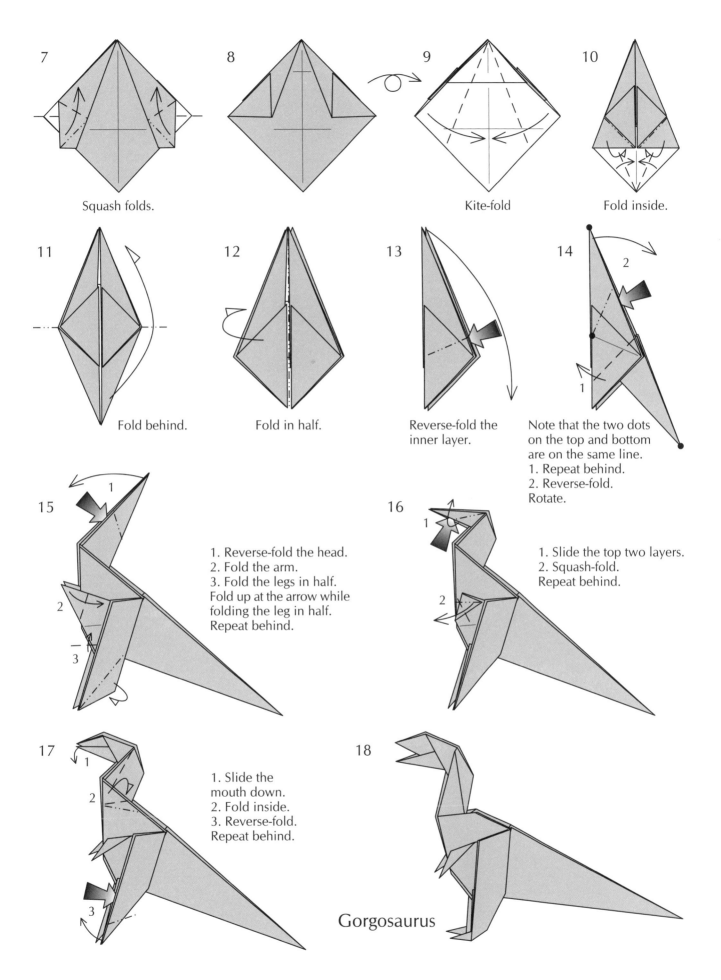

7 Squash folds.

8

9 Kite-fold

10 Fold inside.

11 Fold behind.

12 Fold in half.

13 Reverse-fold the inner layer.

14 Note that the two dots on the top and bottom are on the same line.
1. Repeat behind.
2. Reverse-fold.
Rotate.

15
1. Reverse-fold the head.
2. Fold the arm.
3. Fold the legs in half.
Fold up at the arrow while folding the leg in half.
Repeat behind.

16
1. Slide the top two layers.
2. Squash-fold.
Repeat behind.

17
1. Slide the mouth down.
2. Fold inside.
3. Reverse-fold.
Repeat behind.

18

Gorgosaurus

Protoceratops

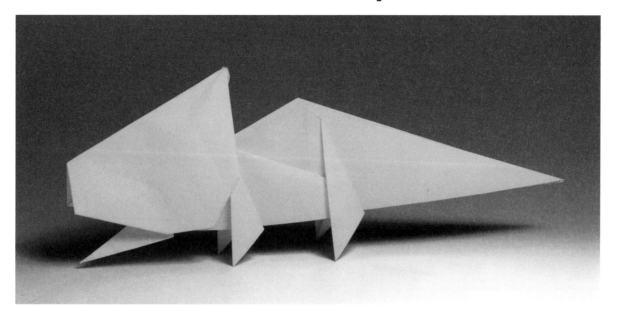

pro-toe-SER-a-tops

Fossils of this Cretaceous dinosaur have been found in Mongolia.

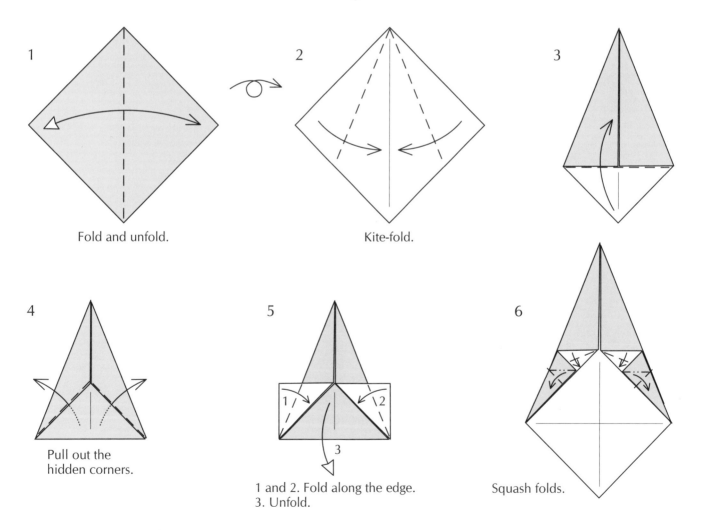

1

Fold and unfold.

2

Kite-fold.

3

4

Pull out the
hidden corners.

5

1 and 2. Fold along the edge.
3. Unfold.

6

Squash folds.

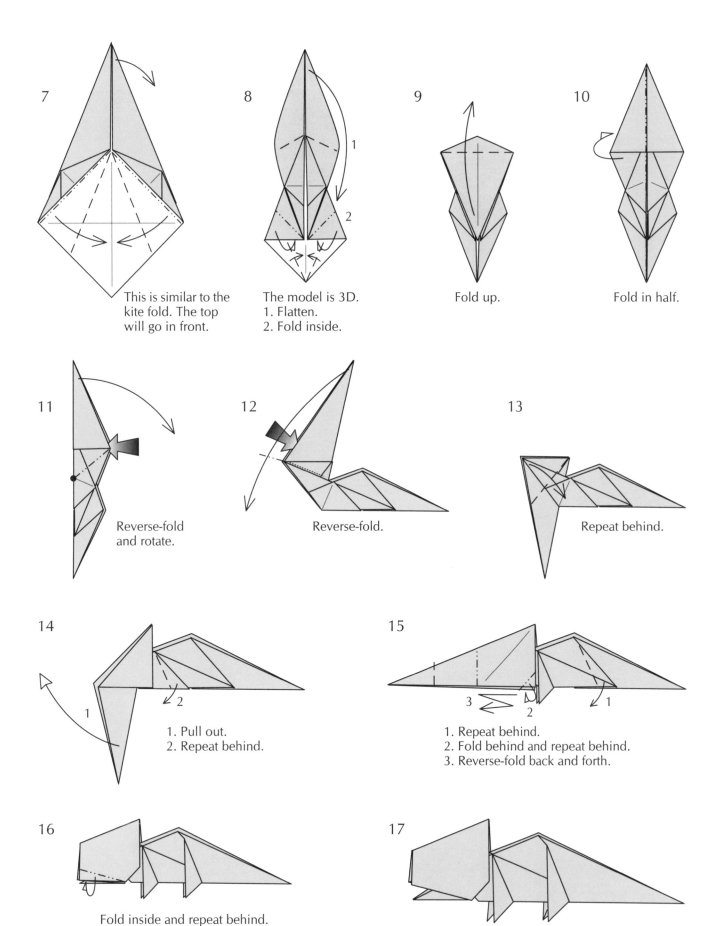

7 This is similar to the kite fold. The top will go in front.

8 The model is 3D.
1. Flatten.
2. Fold inside.

9 Fold up.

10 Fold in half.

11 Reverse-fold and rotate.

12 Reverse-fold.

13 Repeat behind.

14 1. Pull out.
2. Repeat behind.

15 1. Repeat behind.
2. Fold behind and repeat behind.
3. Reverse-fold back and forth.

16 Fold inside and repeat behind.

17

Protoceratops

Triceratops

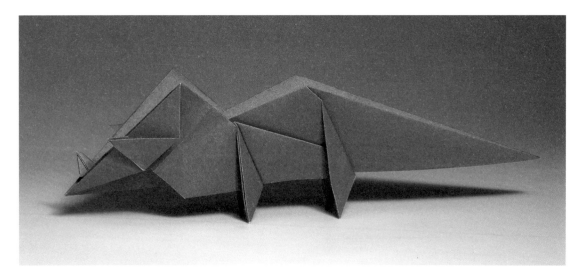

try-SER-a-tops

Western North America was home to this Cretaceous dinosaur.

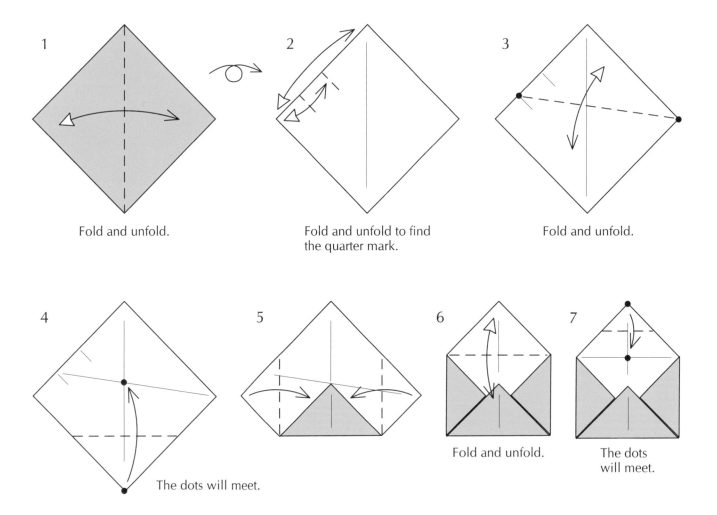

1 Fold and unfold.

2 Fold and unfold to find the quarter mark.

3 Fold and unfold.

4 The dots will meet.

5 The dots will meet.

6 Fold and unfold.

7 The dots will meet.

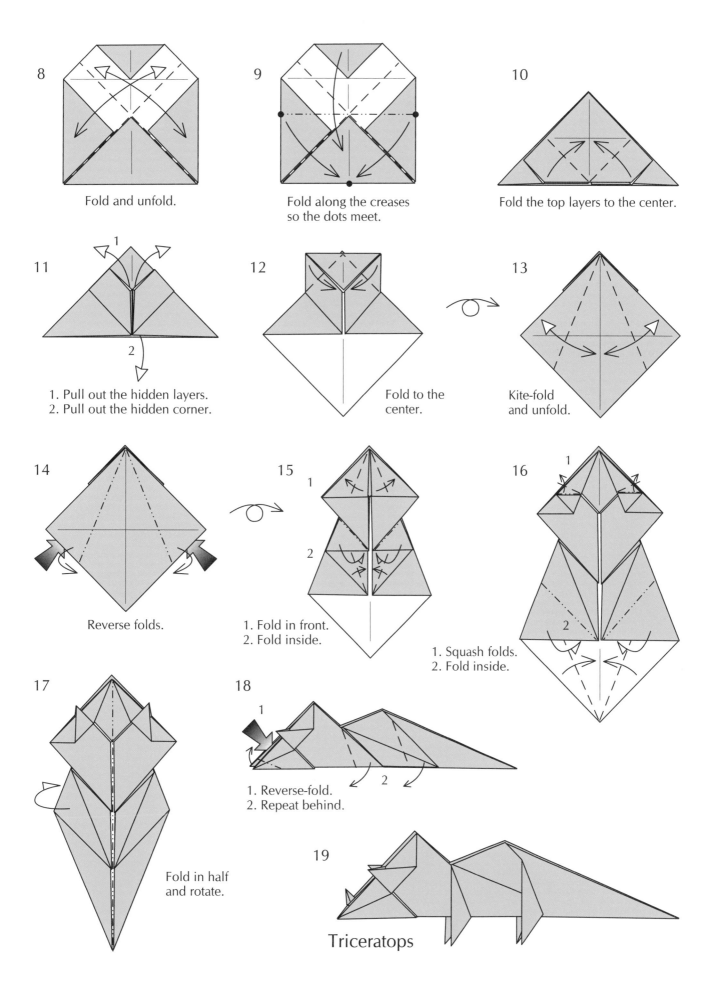

8   Fold and unfold.

9   Fold along the creases so the dots meet.

10   Fold the top layers to the center.

11   1. Pull out the hidden layers.
2. Pull out the hidden corner.

12   Fold to the center.

13   Kite-fold and unfold.

14   Reverse folds.

15   1. Fold in front.
2. Fold inside.

16   1. Squash folds.
2. Fold inside.

17   Fold in half and rotate.

18   1. Reverse-fold.
2. Repeat behind.

19

Triceratops

Stegosaurus

steg-oh-SAWR-us

This Jurassic dinosaur's fossils have been found the Western U.S.

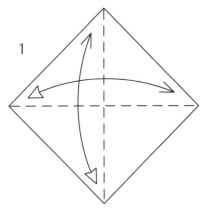

1

Fold and unfold.

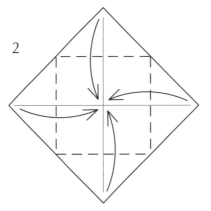

2

Fold to the center.

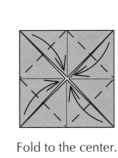

3

Fold to the center.

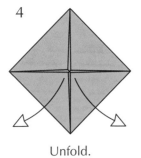

4

Unfold.

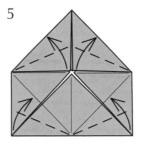

5

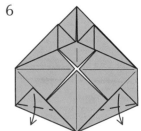

6

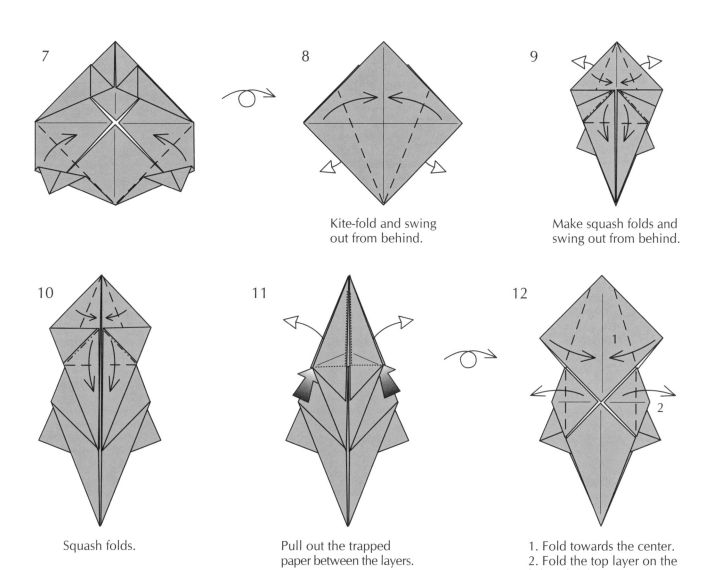

7

8

Kite-fold and swing
out from behind.

9

Make squash folds and
swing out from behind.

10

Squash folds.

11

Pull out the trapped
paper between the layers.

12

1. Fold towards the center.
2. Fold the top layer on the
left and right.

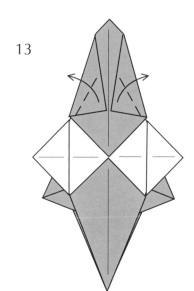

13

Fold the top layer on
the left and right.

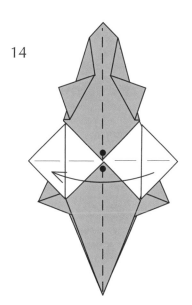

14

Note the flaps with the dots,
they will be folded up in the
next step. Fold in half and rotate.

15

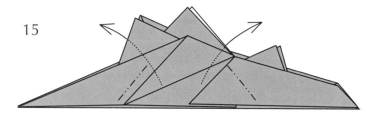

Reverse-fold the hidden corners.

16

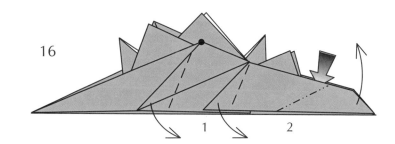

1. Fold the legs and repeat behind.
Fold to the left of the dot.
2. Reverse-fold the head.

17

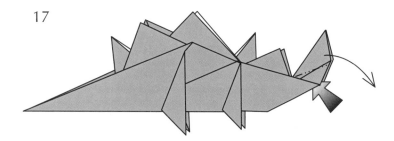

Reverse-fold.

18

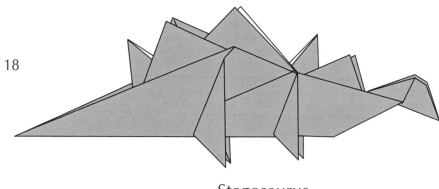

Stegosaurus